The Dark Diary
in 27 refracted moments

poems by

Robert Michael Oliver

Finishing Line Press
Georgetown, Kentucky

The Dark Diary
in 27 refracted moments

Copyright © 2023 by Robert Michael Oliver
ISBN 979-8-88838-235-6 First Edition
All rights reserved under International and Pan-American Copyright Conventions. No part of this book may be reproduced in any manner whatsoever without written permission from the publisher, except in the case of brief quotations embodied in critical articles and reviews.

ACKNOWLEDGMENTS

None of these moments have yet seen the light of day.

I would like to thank my creative life partner, my wife Elizabeth Bruce, for her years of dialogue and support, even in the darkest times; my children Maya and Dylan for their inspirational acts of becoming; the late Robert Hazel whose poetic insights have provided me a lifetime of encouragement; and all the members of my creative community, both current and past, who have nurtured my heart, mind, and soul.

Publisher: Leah Huete de Maines
Editor: Christen Kincaid
Cover Art: Tapestry of Blazing Starbirth, Licensed under the Creative Commons—Attribution 4.0 International; Credit: NASA, ESA, and STScI
Author Photo: Nicolas Ortega Ward
Cover Design: Elizabeth Maines McCleavy

Order online: www.finishinglinepress.com
also available on amazon.com

Author inquiries and mail orders:
Finishing Line Press
PO Box 1626
Georgetown, Kentucky 40324
USA

Table of Contents

Nadir: Beginning ... 1
Dumbfounded ... 2
What Haunts Me ... 3
A Primer: To Invent ... 4
To Invent: A Primer ... 5
Sunday Noon ... 6
A Staccato Affair ... 7
Afterschool Pickup ... 8
Demolition ... 9
No Elegy ... 10
Identity Revealed ... 11
My Habit of Dark ... 12
Waiting for a Glimpse ... 13
To Party or Not ... 14
A Realization over Eggs ... 15
Monday Evening ... 16
Oblivion Removed ... 17
Between Workout and Home ... 18
A Land of Open Spaces ... 19
Curse of Desire ... 20
The End of Cock ... 21
When Humans Cease ... 22
Soul Heavy Sad ... 24
The Moment Between the Hand Wiping the Counter and the
    Lips Sighing ... 25
No Ordinary Hallucination ... 26
What I Left Unsaid ... 27
The Death of Landscapes ... 28

Nadir: Beginning

Again and again,
my eye sought shape.

Again and again,
my ear heard squeal.

Again and again,
my tongue tasted spit.

my nose smelt vile;
my finger pricked.

I now want what
the dog must have.

Dumbfounded

Commitments—how many
must my mind make before
body learns what mind cannot?

I forget myself: this day
repeats. Can the mind not
think what the body wants?

Yesterday, day one.
Today, day one.
Tomorrow, day one.

I become what I repeat:
I leap over cracks; I prance
in heat; rants, I smack!

I repeat what I've become;
the cracks grow deep; the heat
seeps through. I repeat.

What Haunts Me

The candles flicker:
desire stalks my shadow
dancing on a white wall.

I contemplate the dark
wavering on pale skin:
memories molest me.

A Primer: To Invent

I wage against habit,
however iniquitous. Failures
are endemic: thought,

common as a migraine,
familiar as a wife,
astounding as an albatross

soaring above a breeze.
Will this thought wake me
on a sunrise sea? Will I swim

with whales in thick lagoons?
Or will I swell like a multitude
mumbling prayers at dawn?

To Invent: A Primer

To break habit, do
the new, yet never do
that new, again—

Paint the backyard
landing chartreuse!
Paint it now, not

later in the week!
Paint it with cyclones
of lightning, hail!

Paint it!
Paint it mental!
Strip it bare!

Sunday Noon

Out my window
I gaze at her belly
complementing a deck
of hard brown wood,
her bosom bare,
her hair cascading
round her nipple.

I refuse to stare,
yet each dimple,
mole, glistening dew,
like a palm leaf
swaying in a breeze
over a lone atoll,
beacons my lust.

Holding a pillow
to my flesh, a dream
perched above the girl,
sun-dried and tongue
touched, I intone
a void of whispers
wet for her eyes.

A Staccato Affair

We kiss on Mondays
before lunch; her condo,
a block down the road
from my office chair.

She opens the door,
her eyes meet mine.
I adore her swing,
abhor my adoration.

She grins; I smile;
she winks; I smirk;
she grips my palm;
I entwine her fingers.

The blinds slide shut;
her gaze, the throat
of a volcano I leap in,
imagining bliss.

Breathing deeply
I disappear beneath
caresses of fire.
I tilt to the flame.

The lilt on her lips,
her mouth sighing
in exhilaration, closes
mine like a newborn's

on a nipple. I giggle,
my body taut; her
body taut; we taut
till Monday next.

Afterschool Pickup

The girl grips the boy
with her linked fingers,
guides him to a roadside
hovel—exhausted.

Demolition

I hate the sun:
it rises, sets,
brilliantly glowing.

Without the moon,
sun shines.

I hate the dog:
it sleeps, wakes,
hungry for bone.

Without the cat,
dog barks.

I hate the breath:
it forages air,
however heavy.

Without the sneeze
breath breathes—

I hate what is:
independent
of all futures.

Without becoming,
what *is* isn't.

No Elegy

I thought dying
changed the living:
when a lover leaves,

who's left outlasts
the shadow, becomes
as fierce as ash;

but having died,
seen the longing
for the lamented—

long looks across
the room, vacant
as a barrel drained—

hands hold nothing
but the thud of song;
steins hoisted high

clack like fisticuffs
in the hollowed hall
now draped in sash.

What the gone have
touched, the present
touch twice: location

is everything: love,
that space between
kiss and memory,

evaporates like
the aroma of wine
from a waiting tongue.

Identity Revealed

I stroll down the sidewalk,
head up; believe in insurrection;
condemn those who condemn.

The stone I hold is meant
for you; hid, hot as sizzle;
my palm disrupts me.

I won't throw it; promise
passersby with a nod. I have
my own enviable stink.

My Habit of Dark

In winter, my breath fogs
the face seen reflected.

Today, no face, only
that chill that stills

the hand reaching
for a morning cup.

My touch screams halt.
Do I move as the fly

before he is swatted?
I buzz. I do not move.

Swat! If habits are flies,
as relentless as flies,

I might claim victory;
but flies like coyotes

resurrect as anvils fall.
This earth evokes

a tragedy that blames
me for what is,

while blaming fly
for what is not.

Waiting for a Glimpse

I stand cheetah-like
at the garden's edge,
scan the tree line for
white bellied gazelles:

desire has nothing to do
with will. It hunts black,
up-right horns at dusk
as retinas catch the glint

of sharpened enamel.
We'd hunt even if desire
was the discourse of sea
anemones; so, I workout

in gym shorts: phobia
lurching in tennis shoes,
narcissism cross-training
in red t-shirts—a man's

perversion treadmills
until his calendar is full—
then, in a cascading blur,
it begins again at zero.

Like Sisyphus, I
tilt my brow toward
the predawn summit;
I pray for an eclipse.

To Party or Not

I've lost, failed at everything
I wanted, except lying.

I spend an evening with
a pop star, a party born

between thighs and hips;
sculpted knees, I squeeze

as butt presses against
pelvis, tongues lapping

Dewar's—she sucks on
teeth and ice till sunrise.

If nothing lasts, then why
can't Madonna chortle?

Between Workout and Home

At 12:57 p.m.
while cross-training
I knew I had purpose:
I believed in motion.

At 1:23 p.m.
I stride to the exit,
gaze at the banner:
Bold Proud Free!

At 1:24 p.m.
unable to feign—
this threshold holds
no appetite for travel.

I cringe like an eel,
puff up blowfish,
fill the ocean
with my spines!

When smoke rings
fly to a star, we sink
like archipelagos
emanating black.

I might be a bridge
to the future until
passersby discover
I'm disappeared.

I slink from the gym
when the attendant
points her purple nail
at the impossible.

A Land of Open Spaces

Some journeys should never
be taken: the moon's dark side,
the sun's bubbly spot, my own
frown frightened by a freckle.

What can I do but record
the last days of an error?

If I had been Columbus
sailing toward a blue wall
of white gulls, the world would
have discovered me manic;

I would've prayed or be thrown
overboard to certain drowning,

for I've no capacity for dead
reckoning: the sea swells fill
with fault, the falling crests
capsize driftwood rafts.

My journey will end nowhere
long before it ends somewhere.

A Realization over Eggs

I walk to the front door;
wave goodbye to my wife;
the children gobble down
Lucky Charms; my friends
reject my solemn choices;
colleagues, my sanity.

In the dewy light, I am
more ghost than memory:
my pale being an outline
of who I was and what I
might become: a puzzle
piece illuminating Self.

I am but the silhouette
of a phantom designed
to impersonate a man:
I'm poor, without purchase,
unable to eat my eggs
without interrogation.

Monday Evening

Refusing to do
does not defuse
the desire to do.

Excusing what's done
does not defuse
the regret that's done.

I accumulate sin
the way a madame
accumulates johns:

ladies purse their lips,
pouting mouths and hearts
in a simulacrum of lust.

Men settle in flesh
flags and dirty palms;
they wipe their sweat,

acquire rooms to hide
in, closets to bury secrets
beneath piles of garters.

Sleeping in high places,
I can imagine what
the world becomes.

The stories of the dead
outlive me. I have died:
who have I become?

Oblivion Removed

Crude like the sex
of cinema, auto
and savage, non-
negotiable, world-
wasted, frog-legged.

We erect our lives
in stank oblivion,
we build façades
of salt, trenches
in air that dissolve

in a first rainfall:
we rot to the bone,
joints popping, tendon
hanging by gristle in
fleshless revelations.

Then we return
nil consequences,
nil hope, nil all
even the nothing
we once were.

We are a people
without peer, who
hide like a tongue
wanting to speak
only what is silent.

Curse of Desire

I have photographed an erection
with its hat on, tiny tux, ballroom
gown with chiffon wrap, slight
as touch—under spandex:

such images give me pulse, as does
the velvet inversion a woman plants
within her broad, illuminable breath,
lips glistening, drenched in desire.

I know nothing but the debauched:
those acts that pillage, and bruises
swell the brain. "Kiss the world,"
I say, "and the world bites back,"

its breath foul, baked in garlic.
Lips hurting, like broken ribs,
begging for a backhand across
the cheek—again! Without

the slightest obligation,
without the smallest pledge,
this bondage I endure will
twist in rage until affection.

The End of Cock

Let's not deny it!
Let's acknowledge!
Cock will have its way,
in all things Imperial—

Cocks march like storm
troopers donned in pink,
the bitter fist of God
with cracked knuckles.

An intimate rebuttal
requires courage, the kind
battlefields do not teach,
the kind males fail at,

miserably, then even
this procession of cock
camouflaged as morning,
is less than a single cunt.

When Humans Cease

Submerged, what must
I believe? Must I act
like Blake's worm? Am
I Nietzsche's zero?

Dostoevsky understood
the subterranean: a cock
and a cunt—or say penis
and vagina; man, woman

chemically induced beings
with phalluses or vulvas
juking; ovaries (productive),
testes (discreate) gallop

with trumpets blaring,
palms raised in triumph:
in fear, bodies are real,
not hallucinations!

How far can a person be
reduced before becoming
the reduced: name in a log,
a tag on a body bag?

I wish I knew the meaning
of this mind, then I might
bake a cake for my birthday,
hold a gala for a newborn,

weave a tapestry of what
will never be; for this mind
is as chocolate: my mouth
waters, my head rushes

blue demons forth, sings
with joy on crystal meth,
as the mirror captures
what my voice cannot.

Soul Heavy Sad

Nothing out acts the ant:
hoisting caterpillar high,
as light above the leaf,
leaf bends to a breeze.

When I hoist, the floor
groans like the old man
I am, then sags, sore
from the jot of lifting.

Let me touch a face;
let light seep like moon
onto canvas; let it paint
a whisper inside my ear

as midnight sounds
to children at play; they
will count galaxies
till sleep persuades them

to lie down in darkness,
each corpuscle joining
in the hymn of waking.
I do not count. I lift.

The Moment between the Hand Wiping the Counter and the Lips Sighing

The work I do is respite
from work I've not yet done
my long Indian Summer.

When will vestals on vases
cease arousing drudgery?
When will I resign to fate?

I pray for magic to heal
my aching limbs, knees
bruised to the groin.

Ice shakes my chest;
stars vanish in the leer
of infinite potential.

Like a season of hot,
black cats and sweat
remind me of drizzle.

I scrawl an equation in
hieroglyphs I cannot read:
in equal signs, I love.

No Ordinary Hallucination

Bathed in the air of blast furnaces,
touched by the cool of frozen seas,

I exhale the night, and a catalogue
of naught spills a crescent moon

at my feet, white howls fill the sky:
such cities only exist in fiction,

the stardust of cosmic calculations
fraught with rumor and wheel chairs,

crystal refractions and miracle cures.
I am a soul the moment before love

reappears. I touch what is tender,
what might, like a billowing sail

crossing a pitch-black turbulence,
inspire the mind toward speckled sky.

What I Left Unsaid

I stand at the kitchen sink;
the words unchewed I spew
like water bugs on porcelain;
they scatter onto butter knives,
searching for an ear to die in.

Habits require time to unravel:
I have no time: the phone cord
will not untangle itself. Worse,
afterwards, the cord twists again
into an angry strand demanding

attention. I attend, dreaming
a pinafore, yellow as sunset,
billowing swarms of sparrows;
the girl leans against the wall,
revealing her inner thighs.

"If you shake with wonder,
thank morning; with delight,
your lover, the moon is never
full; if you hate, midnight
answers with a sneer."

The Death of Landscapes

Nothing too simple to be true,
too true to be simple, survives
the death of landscapes.

That fertile carrier of hope
now bleak to those who know
better, and want more:

a beating heart; a mammoth's
mind; a palm embracing a pink
cheek; a caress tingling

a shoulder; an epiphany
of firsts; an orchestra of tongues
kissing a baby's foot.

When the universe trembles,
each child quivers, unable to touch
the tomorrow that is dreamt.

Michael's first poem, "The Wolf of the Steps," was inspired by Hermann Hesse's *Steppenwolf*, which was also the first book he ever finished. He was fifteen years old. Since that time his creative endeavors have expanded into theatre, cultural analysis, education, filmmaking, and many other pursuits. Although he has published poems in online journals over the years, *The Dark Diary in 27 refracted moments* marks his return to the public world of poetry makers.

Holding an MFA in Directing and a PhD in Theatre and Performance Studies, Michael co-founded The Sanctuary Theatre in 1983. Its transcultural, multiracial, multiethnic productions, from Derek Walcott's *Ti-Jean and his Brothers* to David Hare's adaptation of William Hinton's *Fanshen*, left an indelible mark on DC's theatre scene during the 1980s. The theatre's production of Egyptian playwright Tawfiq al-Hakim's *The Tree Climber* earned Michael and Sanctuary national recognition.

Later, Sanctuary's The Performing Knowledge Project introduced audiences to original performance pieces, from Elizabeth Bruce's performed short stories, *Legal Tender*, to Michael's poetry-in-performance one-person shows, *Embodying Poe, The Whitman Project: Song of Myself,* and *HOWL in the Time of Trump*, which earned him critical acclaim as a performer and storyteller. Michael was also honored to portray Orson Welles in Auroville, India, in Richard France's *Obediently Yours, Orson Wells*.

In addition to his solo work, Michael's plays have been produced throughout the DC area, most notably, his musical adaptation of George MacDonald's *Wise Woman; Sheepeaters,* done in collaboration with the late South African poet/playwright/performer Mphela Makgoba; and *Ekalavya*, an adaptation of a story from the *Mahabharata*, developed in collaboration with a D.C. Hindi theatre company. His plays have also received many staged readings over the years.

Throughout the last 40 years, Michael has also engaged in a variety of educational opportunities. From high school and university students to older adults and seniors, he has taught a gambit of topics: for high schoolers, courses such as A People's History, Freud and Jung in Literature, and the Theatre of the Oppressed; for university students, dramatic analysis to Professional Writing; for adults, Writers on the Green Line, Acting for Writers, and Performetry; and for seniors, Mementos, poetry writing residences in DC senior centers.

Currently, Michael is finalizing his first novel, *The Green Man and the White House*, and marketing *Thais*, a long-form TV drama that he has developed with several co-creators. He is also putting together the final touches on another book of poetry. Additionally, he recently launched *Creativists in Dialogue*: a podcast embracing the creative life, which he does with Elizabeth Bruce, his wife.

On that note, Elizabeth's third book will be published in 2024, *Universally Adored and Other One Dollar Stories*. They have two wonderful adult children, Maya and Dylan. Finally, Michael's urban garden, which he has planted faithfully for 40 years, supplies the family with tomatoes, peppers, basil, and more.

www.ingramcontent.com/pod-product-compliance
Lightning Source LLC
Chambersburg PA
CBHW022127090426
12713CD00008B/1032